Cambridge English Readers
....
Level 2

Series editor: Philip Prowse

Bad Company

Richard MacAndrew

D1250225

CAMBRIDGE
UNIVERSITY PRESS

CAMBRIDGE UNIVERSITY PRESS
Cambridge, New York, Melbourne, Madrid, Cape Town, Singapore,
São Paulo, Delhi, Dubai, Tokyo, Mexico City

Cambridge University Press
The Edinburgh Building, Cambridge CB2 8RU, UK

www.cambridge.org
Information on this title: www.cambridge.org/9780521179195

First published 2011

Printed in China by Sheck Wah Tong Printing Press Limited

A catalogue record for this publication is available from the British Library

ISBN 978-0-521-17919-5 Paperback
ISBN 978-0-521-17918-8 Book with Audio CD Pack

Typeset by Aptara Inc.
Illustrations by Nick Hardcastle
Map artwork by Malcolm Barnes
Cover image: Getty Images © Gregory Warran 2008

With thanks to Crispin Evans and Bruce Jones

Contents

People in the story

Helen Shepherd: a detective inspector in the police
Brian Webb: a detective sergeant
Dr Atkinson: a police doctor
James McNab: owns McNab Music International (MMI)
Harriet Johnson: sells music for MMI
Claudia Engel: looks after music and musicians for MMI
Ajit Chowdury: looks after MMI's money
Darren Fleming: knew Claudia Engel at university
DC Fox: a detective constable

Places in the story

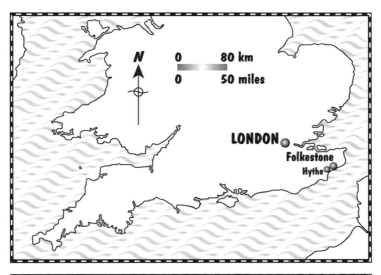

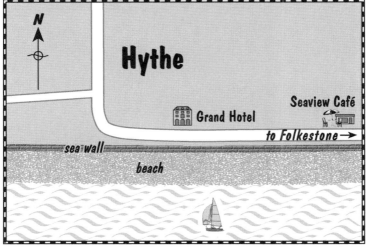

Chapter 1 *A body on the beach*

Noise. Headache. Dry mouth.

Half asleep, Helen Shepherd turned over in bed, but the noise didn't stop. A moment later she woke up.

The noise. It was her phone. She took it off the table next to her bed.

'Yes?' she said. Her dry mouth made it difficult to talk. And her head hurt quite badly. Too much wine last night!

'Is that Detective Inspector Shepherd?' asked a voice.

'Yes,' said Shepherd.

'I'm sorry to wake you,' said the voice. The voice waited for Shepherd to say something, but she didn't. She looked at the clock. It was six thirty.

'Er, well, my name's Webb,' said the voice. 'Brian Webb. I'm your new sergeant. I start working for you today. Well, this morning, actually. Erm … I'm sorry to wake you up, but …'

'Sergeant,' said Shepherd. 'People call me at all times of the day and night. Forget the "sorry". Just tell me what the problem is.'

'There's a body on the beach,' said Webb. 'In Hythe. About two hundred metres from the Grand Hotel. I'm there now.'

'I'll be twenty minutes,' replied Shepherd and put her phone back down on the table.

Shepherd stood under the shower for five minutes. The hot water got the blood moving around her tired body.

She drank half a litre of water and took three aspirins. Five minutes later she was in her car.

The drive from her house in Folkestone to Hythe took Shepherd less than ten minutes. It was the start of autumn and small seaside towns like Hythe were becoming quiet again after the busy summer. The school holidays were over, the beaches were almost empty, and this early in the morning there were few cars on the roads.

As she came into Hythe, Shepherd passed the Seaview Café on her right. It was just opening for breakfast. Two hundred metres down the road, also on the right, she could see a large building – the Grand Hotel. On her left was the sea wall. And on the other side of the wall were the beach and the sea. There were a number of cars by the side of the road. Shepherd stopped behind them.

She looked quickly at herself in the car mirror: grey-blonde hair tied back, intelligent eyes, small nose, thin mouth. 'I don't look too bad,' she thought. But she felt tired and old, and her head still hurt.

She got out of her car and looked over the wall. A cold wind was coming off the sea. The sun was only just up. About fifty metres along the beach some people were standing around and looking down at something. The body.

One of them, a young man in a blue suit, looked round and saw Shepherd.

'That must be Webb,' thought Shepherd. 'He looks about sixteen.'

It was true what people said: as you get older, police officers look younger.

Webb came to meet Shepherd as she walked over.

'I'm Brian Webb, madam,' he said. 'Your new sergeant.'

'I know,' said Shepherd.

'You know?' asked Webb.

'Yes, Sergeant,' replied Shepherd. She waved a hand at the others. 'You're the only person here I don't know, so you must be my new sergeant. I'm a detective, remember.'

'Oh!' said Webb, looking down and then up again.

Shepherd looked him in the eye.

'And don't call me madam,' she said. 'It's Shep. That's what everyone calls me.'

'Right, madam – Shep,' said Webb.

'OK,' said Shepherd. 'Let's go and see what we've got.'

They walked over to the other people. On the beach was the body of a young woman wearing a dark blue skirt, a white blouse and a short red jacket. She had a pretty face and short blonde hair. The back of her head was dark with blood.

A man in white clothes was down on one knee looking at the body. He heard Shepherd arrive and looked up.

'Morning, Shep,' he said.

'Dr Atkinson,' replied Shep.

Atkinson stood up and took the plastic gloves off his hands.

'It's murder,' he said. 'Someone hit her on the back of the head. It killed her.'

'Hit her with what?' asked Shepherd.

'I don't know at the moment,' answered Atkinson. He looked up and down the beach. 'But it could still be here on the beach. Not a stone, I don't think. Something longer. A piece of wood, maybe.'

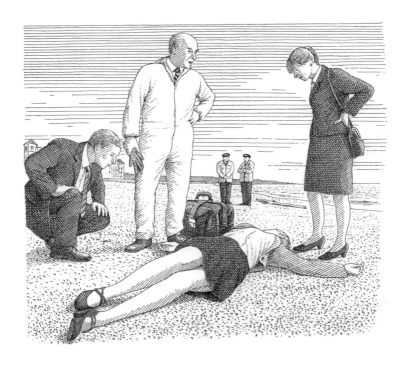

Shepherd looked up and down the beach. There were lots of bits of wood, brought in by the sea.

'What time did she die?' asked Shepherd.

'Late last night or early this morning,' replied Atkinson. 'Say between eleven and two. I can probably tell you more later.'

'OK, thanks,' said Shepherd.

She said nothing for a moment and just looked out to sea. Her head was feeling better already. Three aspirins and a dead body – a quick way to make a headache go away. Not funny really – not for the poor woman dead on the beach.

'Excuse me, ma—, I mean Shep,' said Webb.

Shepherd looked at him. Webb moved uncomfortably from one foot to the other. He was a bit like a young dog, wanting to please her all the time.

'The man who found her ... er, the body,' began Webb. 'He's a waiter at the Grand Hotel and he thinks she was staying there. Well, actually, he's quite sure she was staying there.'

'And where is he now?' asked Shepherd.

'Erm ... he's at the hotel,' replied Webb. 'He had to go to work.'

'What?' said Shepherd, giving Webb an angry look.

'Well ... erm ... he was late already,' replied Webb.

'And what if I want to speak to him?' asked Shepherd. 'Now?'

'Well ...' Webb looked more uncomfortable. 'I can always ...'

'No,' said Shepherd. 'Later. First, I want you to get as many officers as you can down here on the beach. They're looking for the piece of wood or some other thing that killed this woman.'

'Right, Shep,' replied Webb.

Shepherd turned to Dr Atkinson.

'Let the photographer finish his work, then you can take the body away,' she said.

'OK, Shep,' replied Atkinson.

Shepherd walked back up the beach and sat on the top of the sea wall, enjoying the smell of the sea air. She looked in her bag for some cigarettes, then remembered she didn't smoke any more. Three weeks without a cigarette – not bad.

She watched Webb finish his call. 'He must be one of these university police officers,' she thought. 'They leave university, become a police officer, then a sergeant by the age of twenty-five, and know little about real police work.'

Webb walked up the beach to Shepherd.

'Have you worked on many murders before, Sergeant?' asked Shepherd.

'No, Shep,' he replied. 'Not many. Well, not any really.'

'So,' thought Shepherd, 'this could be a difficult job for Webb – his first murder.'

'The first twenty-four hours are the most important,' said Shepherd. 'Don't forget that.'

'Yes. I mean no. I won't,' replied Webb.

'I want the person who did this,' said Shepherd. 'And I want him or her by this time tomorrow. After that our job starts to get more difficult.'

'Right, Shep,' said Webb.

'Now,' said Shepherd. 'You go to the Grand Hotel. Talk to the waiter who found the body. Find out who the dead woman is and what she was doing here. And get us a room where we can talk to people.'

'OK, Shep,' said Webb.

'I'm going over the road for some breakfast,' said Shepherd, looking at the Seaview Café. 'I'll see you at the hotel in half an hour.'

Webb watched Shepherd walk over to the café.

'She wants the job done quickly,' he thought to himself, 'but first she wants breakfast. This could be a long and difficult day.'

Chapter 2   *McNab Music International*

Twenty-five minutes later Shepherd walked through the front doors of the Grand Hotel. She felt much better after a bacon sandwich and a cup of coffee. It was eight o'clock and Webb was waiting for her. There were a number of comfortable sofas and chairs near the front desk, but at this time in the morning not many people were around.

'I've got us a room,' said Webb, leading the way to the back of the hotel. 'It's the Wells room – named after H.G. Wells, the famous writer. Did you know that he lived near here – between Hythe and Folkestone?'

'No,' said Shepherd, her voice uninterested.

Soon they came to a door with the word 'Wells' on it.

Webb opened the door.

'It's not a very large room,' he said. 'The hotel uses it for small meetings and parties.'

'It's fine,' said Shepherd looking round. There was a table in the centre of the room and four chairs down each side of the table.

Shepherd took a chair and waved a hand for Webb to sit down too.

'OK,' she said. 'What have you got?'

'The dead woman is Claudia Engel,' said Webb. He took a piece of paper from inside his jacket and looked at it. 'She's German, but she lived in London. She was here with three other people from a company called MMI – McNab Music International. They're a music company from London.

They use the hotel for meetings from time to time.'

'Who are the others?' asked Shepherd.

Webb looked down at his piece of paper again. 'James McNab. It's his company. Then there's Ajit Chowdury and Harriet Johnson.'

Just then the door opened. A man came into the room and stopped. He was tall, in his early forties, clean-shaven and good-looking. He was well dressed: expensive dark grey suit, clean white shirt and red tie. Shepherd could almost smell the money.

The man looked at Webb, then at Shepherd.

'I'm James McNab,' he said to Shepherd. 'Your sergeant said you wanted to see me.' His voice was rather high for a tall man. 'I asked him why, but he said he couldn't tell me.'

Shepherd got the feeling that this was a man who liked to be the boss. He certainly didn't mind walking into a room without knocking first.

'Well, what's the problem?' said McNab, looking at his watch. 'I've got a meeting at nine o'clock and a lot to do before it.'

With Webb so new to the job, Shepherd couldn't see him asking many questions. She looked at McNab and tried to decide how to begin. 'I'd like him to feel less sure of himself from the beginning,' she thought.

'Does Claudia Engel work for you?' asked Shepherd.

'Yes, she does,' replied McNab. 'And?'

'I'm afraid I've got some bad news,' said Shepherd. 'We found a body on the beach this morning. We believe it is Claudia Engel. We also believe that someone murdered her.'

'What?' McNab's mouth fell open. 'Claudia? I don't believe it. It can't be true.'

'I'm afraid it is,' said Shepherd.

'That's terrible!' said McNab. 'Terrible!'

'I need to ask you some questions,' said Shepherd. 'Take a seat.'

'Well,' said McNab, looking at his watch again. 'Of course, I'll do what I can to help.' He pulled a chair out and sat down.

'Tell me why you're here in Hythe,' said Shepherd.

McNab took a moment to think. He looked at Webb and then at Shepherd.

'Two or three times a year we come here for a day or two,' he began. 'Our offices are in London, but it's sometimes easier to work without the phone going every five minutes. We come here to get away and talk about important business.'

'What important business?' asked Shepherd.

McNab moved on his chair. 'Why do you want to know?' he asked. 'I don't like to tell people too much about our business. Do you need to know this?'

Shepherd put both hands on the table and sat up.

'Mr McNab,' she said quietly, a hard look in her eyes, 'we're talking about a murder. I'm going to ask any question I want and you're going to answer it.'

McNab put both hands up in front of him, as if keeping Shepherd away. 'OK, OK,' he said. 'I was only asking.'

Shepherd sat back.

McNab put his hands down and started speaking again. 'MMI is a music company. We make and sell CDs. We sell music over the internet. We work with musicians. Anything to do with music, we do it – like I say, we're in the music business.'

'So what did you come here to talk about?' asked Shepherd.

'We had to decide a number of things,' replied McNab, but said no more.

Shepherd looked at him. 'Mr McNab,' she said angrily, 'this is going to be much easier if you help me. What things did you have to decide?'

'We have some new bands we're interested in – we wanted to talk about them,' answered McNab, not looking at Shepherd. 'Two of them are very good. And I wanted to talk to the others about where the company is going over the next few years.'

'Tell me about the other people who work for you,' said Shepherd.

McNab looked happier now he was talking about the people in the company and not company business.

'Well, there's Ajit Chowdury,' said McNab. 'He's the money man, the company accountant. Harriet Johnson looks after sales. She sells MMI's music all round the world. And then Claudia looks … looked after the music side of things. The music itself, and the musicians and the bands.'

'And how does everyone get on?' asked Shepherd.

McNab thought for a moment.

'I think we get on well,' he said. 'Of course, we don't always agree with each other, but we're always adult about it. Nobody takes their ball home and says they don't want to play any more, if you see what I mean.'

McNab smiled. Shepherd didn't smile back.

'Tell us about last night,' she said.

'There's not much to tell,' answered McNab. 'We worked until about five. Then we met in the bar some time between seven and seven thirty. We had dinner together in the restaurant and finished about nine thirty. Then we went our different ways. I went to my room and watched TV for half an hour. Then I had a shower and went to bed.'

Shepherd looked at Webb to see if he had any questions.

'Did anything unusual happen yesterday evening?' he asked.

'Good question,' thought Shepherd. 'Maybe there's more to Webb than I thought.'

'No …' began McNab, but then he stopped and thought. 'Actually, yes. There was something strange.'

Webb didn't say anything. He just waited for McNab to speak again.

'When we were in the bar,' said McNab, 'a man came in. As soon as he saw Claudia, he turned round and walked out again – but she saw him. It was very strange. Her face turned white. For a moment she looked terrible. We asked her if she was OK. She said yes, she was fine. She said it was just someone she once knew.'

'What did the man look like?' asked Webb.

'I really don't remember,' said McNab. 'Fair hair, not tall, not short, nothing unusual. I only saw him for a few seconds.'

Shepherd felt it was important to find out more about this man and decided to end the conversation, but McNab was speaking again.

'Inspector,' he said, 'I hope you find this man soon. I mean, I'm sure the news of Claudia's murder will be in the newspapers. But I'd like to keep MMI away from this kind of news as much as I can.'

Shepherd smiled to herself. McNab, the boss, was looking after his company again.

'It'll take as long as it takes, Mr McNab,' she said. 'I'll probably want to talk to you again, after we've spoken to Ms Johnson and Mr Chowdury. I'll also want my officers to look round all your hotel rooms. You can go now, but don't leave the hotel.'

McNab opened his mouth to say something, but then he saw the look in Shepherd's eye. He closed his mouth, looked at Webb, then back at Shepherd.

'Right,' he said.

'Thank you,' said Shepherd.

McNab left the room, closing the door behind him.

Shepherd turned to Webb.

'With people like McNab, you've got to let them know who's the boss,' she said. 'It's us – the police – not them. Don't forget that.'

'Right, Shep,' replied Webb.

'Now,' said Shepherd. 'Harriet Johnson next. But before that, we need to know more about that man who came into the bar last night. Get someone to ask around the hotel. Did anyone see a man – our Mr X – come into the hotel between seven and seven thirty, go into the bar and then leave quickly? If so, who is he? I also want to know when Claudia Engel left the hotel. And was anyone with her?'

'OK,' said Webb. He stood up.

'And we need a look at these people's rooms,' said Shepherd, 'Engel's room and the other three. Two officers to each room. If they find anything strange or unusual, I want to know.'

'Right, Shep,' said Webb, going to the door.

'And, Sergeant?' said Shepherd.

'Yes,' said Webb.

Shepherd looked at her watch. It was too early for a glass of wine.

'Get someone to bring us some coffee.'

Chapter 3   *Questions for Ms Johnson*

Harriet Johnson was wearing black jeans and a pink blouse. She had long dark hair and looked very sure of herself. She sat down in front of Shepherd and Webb.

'James told me the news,' she said. 'I understand you want to talk to me.'

'Yes,' said Shepherd slowly, giving Johnson a long look. 'How well did you know Ms Engel?'

'Well enough,' replied Johnson. 'We worked together for two years.'

Shepherd gave her another long look. Something was wrong.

'You don't look sad,' said Shepherd.

Johnson gave a short laugh.

'No, I don't, do I?' she said. Her mouth smiled, but not her eyes. 'Well, I didn't like Claudia Engel at all. Actually, I hated her.'

Shepherd looked questioningly at Johnson.

'The old, old story,' said Johnson, again with a short laugh. 'I had a boyfriend. She took him away from me. They started going out while I thought he and I were still together. Then I found out what was happening. He left me for her – well, I told him not to come back actually. Then later she left him.'

'I see,' said Shepherd.

'She made me very unhappy. Then she made my boyfriend unhappy. Mind you, he never really did know what he wanted anyway. This all happened two years ago, when she started at MMI. It all meant nothing to her. But it didn't mean nothing to me.'

'And you hated her,' said Shepherd.

'I did,' said Johnson. 'I probably still do.'

'Yes,' thought Shepherd. 'You do.' She could almost feel the hate coming across from the other side of the table.

'But I didn't kill her,' said Johnson.

'How did the others feel about Engel?' asked Shepherd. 'McNab, Chowdury.'

Johnson smiled again. 'They didn't like her much,' she answered. 'Ajit Chowdury wanted her job. OK, he's the

accountant, but he thinks he knows a lot about music. He doesn't want to sit in an office all day. He wants to be out and about with famous musicians.'

'And McNab?' asked Shepherd.

'Dear old James,' answered Johnson. 'He likes everyone to think he's the boss, doesn't he? But, actually ... well, he's just a little bit afraid of women. You probably saw that, Inspector.'

For a moment Shepherd thought about smiling, but decided against the idea.

'Anyway,' Johnson was speaking again, 'he was certainly afraid of Claudia. Over the last two years she was the real brains behind the company. The musicians loved her. She knew what music the public wanted to buy. And James knew he just had to agree to her ideas.'

'How long have you worked for MMI?' asked Shepherd.

'Fifteen years,' answered Johnson. 'Since James started the company.'

'And the company is doing well?' asked Shepherd.

'Fine,' replied Johnson quickly. Too quickly maybe, thought Shepherd.

'Some of our musicians are big names all over the world,' said Johnson. 'And we're taking on two new bands. I haven't heard them, but people say they're excellent.'

'Tell us about last night,' said Shepherd.

Johnson told Webb and Shepherd about the four of them having drinks in the bar.

'Then we had dinner,' said Johnson. 'We finished about nine thirty.'

'McNab told us about a man who came into the bar. Someone Claudia Engel knew,' said Shepherd. 'You haven't told us about him.'

'I didn't see him,' replied Johnson. 'I had my back to the door, and by the time I turned round, he was gone.'

'But you're sure Ms Engel knew him?' Shepherd made it a question.

'Oh yes,' said Johnson. 'The look on her face told me that. Actually, I think she met him later. She certainly met someone.'

Shepherd looked questioningly at Johnson.

'After dinner I sat in the lounge, had a coffee and read a book,' began Johnson. 'While I was there, Claudia came down from her room and went out of the front doors. From where I was sitting I could see through the doors – they're glass – and she was standing there. Outside. Waiting. I'm sure she was waiting for someone. Then she walked away to the left. It was as if she could see the person she was meeting.'

'Why did you think that?' asked Shepherd.

'Just the way she was walking,' said Johnson.

'But you didn't see the person she was meeting?' asked Shepherd.

'No,' said Johnson. 'It was too dark.'

'What time was this?' asked Shepherd.

'Probably about ten thirty,' answered Johnson. 'Maybe ten forty-five. I went up to my room soon after that.' She moved uncomfortably on her chair.

'And you didn't see Ms Engel again?' asked Shepherd.

'No,' replied Johnson.

Shepherd looked at Webb.

'There's salt on your shoes,' he said to Johnson.

'What do you mean?' asked Johnson.

'They're white round the bottoms,' said Webb. 'That's salt. From the sea. Have you been on the beach?'

Shepherd looked at Johnson's shoes. They were black trainers. And there was salt round the bottom of them.

'Not bad, Webb,' she thought.

'Well, I went for a walk on the beach yesterday afternoon,' replied Johnson.

'Yesterday afternoon?' Webb made it a question.

'Yes,' replied Johnson.

'You didn't go out again in the evening? After ten thirty perhaps?' asked Webb.

'No,' answered Johnson, her voice not as strong as before. 'I've told you. I went up to my room.'

Webb said nothing. He just looked at Johnson.

Shepherd could see Johnson's face beginning to go a little red. Maybe there was something she didn't want the police to know.

Johnson moved uncomfortably on her chair again. 'I've told you,' she said again. 'I went up to my room.'

Webb looked at Shepherd.

'OK, Ms Johnson,' said Shepherd. 'You can go. We'll want to talk to you again, so don't leave the hotel. OK?'

'Right,' said Johnson quietly, and she left the room, head down.

Shepherd and Webb looked at each other.

'She wasn't very happy about something, was she?' said Shepherd.

'There's something she's not telling us,' answered Webb. 'Or maybe she just didn't like my questions.'

Shepherd stood up.

'I need some air,' she said, taking her bag off the back of the chair. 'And I've got a call to make. Go and see if there's any news about our Mr X or from the officers in the rooms. I'll be outside the front of the hotel.'

* * *

Fifteen minutes later Shepherd was standing outside the front doors of the hotel. Her phone was in her hand.

Webb came out of the hotel at a fast walk. He had a piece of paper in his hand.

'Two things, Shep,' he said.

Shepherd closed her phone. 'Well?' she asked.

'We know who Mr X is,' said Webb, looking pleased with himself. 'And one of the receptionists agrees with Johnson that Engel left the hotel at ten thirty. But she also saw Chowdury leave the hotel at about ten forty-five.'

Chapter 4   *How well is MMI doing?*

Shepherd waited for Webb to say more, but he didn't. 'He probably wants me to say, "Well done,"' she thought.

'Come on. Don't just stand there. Tell me,' she said.

Webb looked uncomfortable. His face went a little red. He looked at the piece of paper in his hand.

'Well … erm … the man's called Darren Fleming. We talked to some of the people who work in the bar. He comes into the hotel for a drink from time to time. He lives in Hythe somewhere. We're trying to find him now.'

'Right,' said Shepherd. 'When you do, bring him here. What about Chowdury?'

Webb looked at the paper in his hand again.

'Do you always write things down?' asked Shepherd. 'Do you have problems remembering?'

'No, Shep,' said Webb, smiling a little, but still looking rather uncomfortable. He waved the paper at her. 'Someone gave me this. Detective Constable Fox I think his name is.'

'All right, all right,' said Shepherd. She preferred not to think about DC Fox. Fox loved writing everything down, putting everything in the right place, doing everything just right. Not Shepherd's sort of person at all.

'I know he's a lot older than you,' said Shepherd. 'But don't take too many lessons from Fox.'

'I'll try not to,' replied Webb.

For a moment Webb thought he saw the start of a smile on Shepherd's face, but then it was gone.

'The receptionist remembered Chowdury leaving the hotel at about ten forty-five last night,' said Webb. 'He was dressed in running clothes.'

Shepherd thought for a moment. 'OK,' she said. 'Get Ajit Chowdury. We'll have a talk with him next.'

She put her phone away in her bag. 'I've just been on the phone to a friend of mine in London,' she told Webb. 'She told me some interesting things about MMI. I hope the company accountant has some good answers.'

* * *

Twenty minutes later Chowdury was sitting in the Wells room in front of Shepherd and Webb. It was ten thirty. Chowdury was a tall good-looking man in his early thirties. He had on a dark brown suit, cream shirt and light brown tie. His fingers were playing with the front of his jacket; his eyes were looking from Shepherd to Webb and back again.

'Softly, softly,' thought Shepherd. 'Don't make him uncomfortable, or he won't say anything. Start with some easy questions.'

'Tell us about your job, Mr Chowdury,' she began.

Chowdury sat back in the chair and stopped playing with his jacket. 'I'm the company accountant. I look after the money,' he answered, smiling a little.

'So I understand,' said Shepherd. 'And is it a good job? A good company to work for?'

'Well, yes. I think so,' he replied.

'Do you all like each other? I mean, do you work well together?' asked Shepherd.

'We aren't all great friends,' he replied. 'But we work well together. Yes.'

'Claudia Engel too?' asked Shepherd quietly.

Chowdury looked away to one side for a moment then back at Shepherd. 'She could be rather difficult,' he said.

'Tell me about it,' said Shepherd. 'Believe me, I know all about working with difficult people.'

Chowdury gave her a small smile. 'She was a hard woman,' he began. 'She knew what she wanted. She knew how to get it. And she didn't allow anybody to get in her way.'

'I understand you know quite a bit about music,' said Shepherd, 'as well as money.'

'Yes,' replied Chowdury. 'But Claudia never listened to what I thought. I spend a lot of time in clubs. I've seen a lot of good new bands. But she always knew best.'

There was something strange in Chowdury's voice that made Shepherd ask her next question.

'Were you lovers?' she asked.

Webb turned quickly to look at Shepherd.

There was fire in Chowdury's eyes. 'It's nothing to do with …' he started.

'It's murder,' said Shepherd, her voice hard, before Chowdury could finish.

Chowdury's head went down. Then he looked at her again. 'We slept together once,' he said, an angry look in his eyes. 'And then she said that was it. It was over. Finished.'

'And that made you angry,' said Shepherd. It wasn't a question.

'It still does,' said Chowdury. 'But not enough to kill her. It hurt me at the time, but it was just one night. And she didn't tell everyone about it. No-one in the office knew.'

'Did she like working for McNab?' asked Shepherd.

'When she started, she was quite happy,' began Chowdury, 'but things have been difficult for the last month or two.'

'In what way?' asked Shepherd.

'Well, at first she and James always agreed on everything,' replied Chowdury. 'But, like I said, for the last month or two they haven't. I was walking past McNab's room yesterday afternoon – we're all on the second floor – and I could hear her in there. They were shouting at each other.'

'What about?' asked Shepherd.

'I didn't hear much,' answered Chowdury. 'One of the hotel cleaners was near, so I couldn't stop and listen. But I did hear her say, "You need me, James. Give me what I want, or your company is finished." That was all I heard.'

'What do you think she wanted?' asked Shepherd.

'Money.' Chowdury didn't stop to think for a moment.

'Ah!' said Shepherd, thinking about the telephone conversation with her friend in London.

'And how is the company doing?' asked Shepherd. 'I've heard it's not doing too well.'

'Who told you that?' asked Chowdury quickly.

'How is the company doing?' Shepherd asked again, her voice a little harder.

Chowdury thought for a moment.

'Not great,' he said. 'I mean, I'm the accountant. I can make the numbers look good on paper, but actually they're not great. Some of our big stars aren't as good as they were. Sales fell last year and will fall again this year. There are two new bands out there that we think are very good. Claudia was trying to get them to work with MMI, but they're still thinking about it.'

'I see,' said Shepherd. She said nothing for a moment.

Then Webb spoke. 'What about last night?' he asked. 'Where were you going at about a quarter to eleven?'

'For a run. Why?' asked Chowdury.

'Which way did you go?' asked Webb.

'Out of the hotel and right,' replied Chowdury. 'I ran along by the beach for four or five kilometres and then came back. I got back about eleven thirty.'

Shepherd thought, 'Claudia Engel's body was a few hundred metres to the left of the hotel. The other way.'

At that moment DC Fox's head came round the door.

'Shep,' he said. 'You'll want to see this.'

Shepherd left the room for a moment and then came back in. Fox stood by the door. In Shepherd's hand was a golf club in a long plastic bag.

'One of my officers found this in your room,' she said to Chowdury. 'Is it yours?'

Chapter 5 *More about Claudia Engel*

Chowdury opened his mouth and closed it again.

'Yes, it's mine,' he said.

'You only have one golf club?' asked Shepherd.

'It's a new one,' answered Chowdury. 'I bought it the day before yesterday. My other clubs are in the golf bag in the back of my car.'

'We'll need to look at those too,' said Shepherd, putting out a hand. 'Keys, please.'

Chowdury gave his car keys to Shepherd. She passed his keys and the golf club to Fox.

'You know what to do,' she said.

'Yes, Shep,' Fox replied.

Shepherd looked at her watch, then at Chowdury.

'You can go,' she said, 'but don't leave the hotel. I'll have more questions for you later.'

Chowdury left the room.

Webb looked at Shepherd. 'Your phone call,' he said. 'That's how you know business is not good.'

'Yes,' replied Shepherd. 'A friend in the music business. It's a small world.'

'And how did you know that Chowdury and Engel were lovers at one time?' Webb asked.

'I didn't,' said Shepherd. 'But there was something in his voice that made me think it was a good question to ask.'

Shepherd took a pen from the table and started playing with it. 'And DC Fox told me that Darren Fleming is here.

Get him in here next. Ask for some sandwiches for later too. And more coffee, if you want it.'

Shepherd looked at her watch. It was twelve o'clock. Time for a real drink.

'And you can get me a glass of red wine from the bar,' she said.

Webb looked at Shepherd as he stood up. She was certainly different from other police inspectors he knew.

But he just said, 'Right, Shep.'

'And this time you ask the questions,' said Shepherd.

Webb smiled.

'Thanks.'

'Don't thank me yet,' replied Shepherd, not smiling back. 'I'll be in here with you.'

* * *

A few minutes later, they were back in the Wells room. Shepherd and Webb were in their usual seats; Darren Fleming was opposite them. Fleming was in his late twenties, wearing jeans and a brown shirt.

'Why am I here?' he asked Shepherd.

'You were in the hotel last night,' said Webb.

'Yes, but only for a short time,' answered Fleming.

'Why was that?' asked Webb.

'Because I saw someone …' began Fleming. He stopped. He looked at Shepherd, then back at Webb. 'What's all this about?' he asked.

'We found a body on the beach early this morning,' said Webb. 'Claudia Engel's body. She was dead.'

'Murdered?' asked Fleming.

'Yes,' said Webb.

'Poor Claudia,' said Fleming. 'Poor Claudia.'

'You knew her?' asked Webb.

'Yes. We were students together in London,' said Fleming. 'We lived in the same house. For a year. Not happy times.'

'Why not?' asked Webb.

'It was an unhappy house – mainly because of Claudia,' said Fleming. He was quiet for a moment, remembering. Then he spoke again.

'We were studying the same thing – business – so I saw a lot of her. She wasn't a nice person. When she said something, you never knew if it was true. She sometimes told stories about people – other students – and I knew the stories were untrue. She could be really nice if she wanted something – help with her studies, someone to cook her a meal – but you had to do what she wanted. If you didn't, she told everyone else how terrible you were. By the end of the year I just wanted to get out of that house. There were five of us living there and everyone felt the same way.'

'Did she know how you felt?' asked Webb.

'Oh yes,' said Fleming. 'She certainly knew how I felt. One time she wanted to borrow a piece of my work. She wanted to use it in something she was doing. I wasn't having any of it. I told her no. She could do her own work. She said some bad things about me to other people and I found out.'

'And?' asked Webb.

'I told her what I thought of her. In front of most of the students from one of our classes. I was so angry.'

Then Fleming smiled. 'But that was ten years ago,' he said.

'And are you still angry?' asked Webb. 'Because you just turned round and walked out of the hotel last night.'

Fleming sat up in his chair and looked at Webb.

'No,' he said. 'I'm not angry now. If anything, I feel sorry for her. She had no real friends. But yes, I walked out last night. The past is sometimes a dangerous place. I didn't want to go there. I went back home. I was unlucky enough to see Claudia Engel for about five seconds yesterday evening. That's all. I didn't see her again. Now can I go?'

'You didn't meet her later that evening?' asked Webb.

'Certainly not,' replied Fleming.

'Was anyone with you when you were at home?' asked Webb.

'No,' replied Fleming.

'Did you phone anyone? Email anyone?' asked Webb.

'No,' replied Fleming.

Webb looked at Shepherd.

'Put all this in writing for one of my officers,' Shepherd told Fleming. 'Then you can go. But don't leave Hythe.'

* * *

Ten minutes later Shepherd and Webb were standing outside the front doors of the hotel. Webb had a sandwich, Shepherd her glass of wine.

'What a nice young woman Claudia Engel was!' said Shepherd.

Webb smiled.

Shepherd drank some wine.

'Good questioning in there,' she said.

'Thank you,' said Webb.

'Don't get too pleased with yourself,' said Shepherd. 'We've still got a long way to go.'

Webb smiled to himself. 'By the way, Shep,' he began, 'there's a door at the back of the hotel where you could go out without anyone seeing you.'

'Right,' said Shepherd. 'That's good to know.'

Shepherd thought for a moment.

'Let's go and have a look round Engel's room,' she said. 'I know DC Fox has been there already, but I want to see it for myself. Fox is a good officer, but sometimes he's too careful. He doesn't let his brain run free. Get the key from reception and meet me on the second floor.'

* * *

A few minutes later Webb met Shepherd outside Claudia Engel's room.

'Reception gave me a key, but it isn't Engel's,' said Webb as he opened the door. 'No-one can find her key and it wasn't on the body.'

'Oh,' said Shepherd, 'that's interesting.'

Claudia Engel had a large double room looking over the sea.

'I'll start in the bathroom,' said Shepherd. 'You look round here.'

'What are we looking for?' asked Webb.

'We'll know it when we see it,' answered Shepherd.

Shepherd took a quick look round the bathroom. There wasn't much to see – Engel was only staying two or three nights. Shepherd saw nothing unusual. She went back into the bedroom.

Webb was looking through Engel's clothes.

'Anything?' asked Shepherd.

'No, Shep,' answered Webb.

Shepherd looked round the room. There was a book, a clock and a music magazine on the table next to the bed. Some keys on the table too – house and car, thought Shepherd. A raincoat behind the door – nothing in the pockets.

She looked round the room again. Something was wrong. She didn't know what. She could feel her morning headache coming back, just when she didn't need it.

Just then she heard Webb's phone. He answered it.

Shepherd looked out of the window at the sea, not listening to Webb's conversation, but thinking about the room. What was wrong with it? And where was Engel's key? She heard Webb finish his conversation.

Shepherd looked at Webb.

'Well?' she asked.

'Nothing important,' replied Webb.

Shepherd looked round the room a third time.

'You know I said, "We'll know it when we see it,"' she began.

'Yes?' said Webb questioningly.

'Well, we'll also know it if we don't see it,' said Shepherd.

'What do you mean?' asked Webb. Then he smiled. 'Oh, I see. So what have we not found – other than the key?'

'The thing that business people all around the world carry with them at all times,' said Shepherd.

'A laptop computer,' replied Webb.

'Let's start again,' said Shepherd.

Five minutes later they were finished. There wasn't a laptop in the room – not in the cupboard, not under the bed, not in the bed, nowhere.

'We need to find it,' said Shepherd. 'First, find out if she had one here – I can't believe she didn't – and find out what sort it was. Then put all our officers on it. Look all round the hotel. Have another look in the rooms of those other three jokers – McNab, Johnson and Chowdury. Send someone round to Fleming's house. And get as many people as you can to go along the beach again.'

'Right, Shep,' said Webb.

'After that, you'll find me in the bar,' said Shepherd.

Chapter 6   *Unanswered questions*

At two o'clock Webb found Shepherd, sitting at the bar, talking to the barman. She looked round as Webb came in. The barman moved away.

'Engel had a laptop,' said Webb, sitting next to her. 'We know what sort it is. I've got all our officers looking for it.'

'Good,' said Shepherd. 'Now, there are a number of things I want to know. For a start, what's on Engel's laptop? Second, why did Engel think that MMI needed her so much? Remember what Chowdury heard her say – "Give me what I want, or your company is finished." What could she do to bring an end to the company? Next, what's Harriet Johnson not telling us? She was very uncomfortable about some of our questions. And last, why do McNab and Johnson say that the business is doing well when Chowdury says it isn't, and my friend in the music business knows it isn't?'

Shepherd waved at the barman. 'I'll have a glass of red wine, please,' she said.

Webb gave Shepherd a funny look. Shepherd saw it.

'When you've done this job as long as I have, Sergeant,' she said, 'you'll find you need a glass of red wine now and then.'

'While you're working?' asked Webb.

'It helps me think,' replied Shepherd.

A grey-haired man came into the room and stood at the far end of the bar. He put his keys on top of the bar and waited for the barman to come over.

DC Fox came to the door and waved.

'See what he wants,' said Shepherd and stayed sitting. Webb left the room to talk to Fox.

Shepherd sat and thought. She looked at the grey-haired man, now sitting at the other end of the bar. Then she looked at his keys. There were four or five. And something else. What was it? Oh yes! A memory stick for a computer.

Webb came back. 'They've found Engel's room key and her laptop,' he told Shepherd. 'They were hidden in an old garage at the back of the hotel. But I don't think we're going to get anything from the laptop. Someone's broken it up. It was in pieces. And I'm not sure we've got all the bits.'

Shepherd put her head in her hands for a moment. Then she looked up and saw the memory stick on the bar again. It gave her an idea.

'Wait a minute,' she said. She looked out of the window, and thought for a minute. Then she looked at Webb. 'I've had an idea.' She thought for a few moments more, a finger to her mouth, her eyes half closed.

'OK. Let's do it,' said Shepherd. 'I want to see McNab, Johnson and Chowdury in the Wells room. Fleming too. Send a car for him. Let's say we'll meet in forty-five minutes. I've got a few things to do first.'

'Right, Shep,' said Webb and left the room, asking himself what her idea could be.

Shepherd sat for a few minutes, thinking through her idea. Then she left too, taking her wine with her.

* * *

It was four thirty by the time Webb got everyone together in the Wells room. Shepherd walked in and looked round. Webb was already sitting in his usual place. Across the table sat Chowdury, McNab and Johnson. Fleming sat a little away from the table. DC Fox stood just inside the door.

'Good afternoon, everyone,' said Shepherd. 'This is Mr Fleming.' She waved a hand at Fleming. 'You will know him from last night. He knew Ms Engel some years ago.' She looked at Fleming. 'Over here are Mr McNab, Ms Engel's

boss, and Mr Chowdury and Ms Johnson, who worked with Ms Engel.'

Shepherd walked round the table. There was an envelope in her hand, which she put on the table in front of her chair. Then she sat down.

'I've asked you all here together because one of you killed Claudia Engel,' said Shepherd.

Everyone started speaking at the same time. Shepherd put up a hand.

'Stop talking,' she said. Everyone stopped speaking.

'I don't know how many friends Ms Engel had,' began Shepherd, 'but certainly no-one here was friends with her.'

McNab started to say something, but Shepherd put up a hand again.

'Later, Mr McNab,' she said. 'You can say something later.'

'Not one of you liked her. Each of you could be the killer. Mr Fleming, you say you were at home, but we don't know if that's true. Mr Chowdury, you say you turned right for a run along the beach, but what if you went the other way? Ms Johnson, you say you sat in the lounge and then went to your room, but what if you went outside? And Mr McNab, you say you watched TV in your room and then went to bed, but how do we know that?'

Shepherd saw Johnson look at McNab and move on her seat.

'Now look here—' said McNab.

'Shut up,' said Shepherd. She looked at the four faces in front of her, then at McNab.

'MMI isn't doing well, is it?' she said. 'And don't try and tell me it is.'

McNab gave Chowdury an angry look.

'I didn't tell her,' said Chowdury. 'She knew already.'

McNab looked back at Shepherd.

'How ...' he began.

'Is it?' said Shepherd.

'No, it isn't,' said McNab. 'But there are these two new bands ...'

'Ah, yes!' said Shepherd. 'The two bands. Are they real?'

'Yes,' said McNab and Chowdury at the same time.

'Good,' said Shepherd. 'Now have I got this right? If these two bands come to MMI, your company is OK. But if these two bands go to a different company, then that's the beginning of the end for MMI. Is that right?'

'Well ...' began McNab.

'Yes,' said Chowdury. 'He'll try and tell you something different, but MMI is just a small company. It can't get much smaller.'

'So, if the bands don't come to you, that's the end of MMI. And you all lose your jobs,' said Shepherd. 'And the person who was bringing the bands to MMI was Claudia Engel.'

'What are you saying?' asked McNab.

'I'm not saying anything,' said Shepherd. 'I'm just making sure we all understand where we are.'

She looked round the room at everyone again.

'The next thing I want to talk about is Ms Engel's laptop,' she said. 'We've just found it. In pieces. Hidden in an old garage at the back of the hotel.'

At that moment the door opened. A police officer said something to DC Fox. Fox came over to Shepherd and spoke to her quietly. She looked at Johnson.

'Just what I need,' thought Shepherd. A way to make Harriet Johnson talk.

'Ms Johnson, one of the cleaners saw you leaving the hotel this morning at six thirty. You were carrying a laptop bag. Perhaps you could tell us what you were doing.'

Chapter 7   *Who killed Claudia Engel?*

Everyone in the room looked at Harriet Johnson.

'I …' began Johnson. Her face turned dark red. She stopped and then started again.

'I was taking my laptop out to my car,' she said. 'This was our last day here. I knew I didn't need my laptop again, so I went to put it in my car. But it was my laptop. You have to believe me.'

'Excuse me, Shep.' It was Fox who spoke. 'When we asked to see everyone's laptop, Ms Johnson's was in her room.'

'Yes, yes,' said Johnson. 'I know. I brought it back. When I knew we had to stay longer because of … because of Claudia, I went and got it. I thought I could do some work.'

Shepherd looked at Johnson for a few seconds. 'Tell me, Ms Johnson,' she began, her voice hard, 'tell me everything that you did after ten thirty last night.'

For a moment Johnson didn't speak. She looked at McNab, then at Shepherd.

'And don't tell me you just went to your room and went to bed,' said Shepherd, 'because I won't believe you.'

Johnson looked down at her hands for a moment and then up at Shepherd.

'I went to James's room,' she said. 'I wanted to ask him something about a problem we're having with sales in North America. I needed to send an email to the States before I went to bed. But James wasn't there. He didn't come to the door.'

Johnson looked at McNab. 'I'm sorry, James,' she said.

'Well, Mr McNab?' asked Shepherd. 'Where were you?'

Now McNab's face went red.

'I was probably in the shower,' he answered. 'I told you I had a shower before I went to bed.'

'You didn't go out?' said Shepherd. 'You didn't use the door at the back of the hotel?'

'No,' he replied.

Shepherd looked round the room at everyone. Her fingers started playing with the envelope on the table in front of her. The envelope was open and there was writing on the front of it. She looked back at James McNab.

'Maybe what you're saying is true; maybe it's not,' said Shepherd. 'I don't know yet, but one way or another I'm going to find out.' She looked round the room again. 'And I do know this. Claudia Engel's laptop is important. Her killer knows it's important too. There's something on her computer – an email, a letter, something like that – something that will tell me who the killer is.'

Nobody spoke. The room was very quiet.

'I also think Ms Engel knew she was in danger,' said Shepherd, looking in turn at each of the people sitting in front of her. She turned the envelope over so that everyone could see the writing on the front. There were two words: 'Claudia Engel'.

'She left this at the hotel reception yesterday afternoon,' said Shepherd, opening the envelope and turning it over. A memory stick fell out onto the table in front of her. 'Do you know what's on this?' she asked and then answered the question herself. 'Everything that was on her computer. Claudia put everything important from her laptop onto this memory stick and gave it to reception to keep safe. It could take me some time to find what I'm looking for – the important email or letter – but I will find it.'

Again nobody spoke. Shepherd watched everyone carefully. Johnson's hand went to her mouth. Chowdury looked like he had a lot of questions to ask. Fleming was sitting back in his chair looking from Shepherd to the MMI people and back again. But it was McNab who looked most uncomfortable.

Shepherd watched him carefully.

At that moment the door opened. A police officer gave DC Fox a piece of paper. Fox passed the paper to Shepherd, who looked at it, then smiled at Webb. Webb looked at her questioningly. Shepherd looked round the room again.

'You'll be interested to know that one of my officers has had a look at the door at the back of the hotel,' she said. 'He's found quite a few fingerprints on it from a number of different hands. We've also found the piece of wood used to hit Ms Engel, and we're looking for fingerprints on that. But then, of course, I'm sure the murderer wore gloves …'

She stopped speaking for a moment and watched McNab. All the colour left his face.

'… or maybe not,' finished Shepherd.

McNab's mouth opened and closed. He started to speak, then stopped, then started again.

'Yes, Mr McNab?' said Shepherd quietly.

'I had to,' he said. 'I just had to. She wanted too much. She always wanted too much. She earned good money, but she wanted double.'

'And you didn't want to pay that,' said Shepherd.

'I couldn't,' said McNab. 'I couldn't, but she didn't believe me. "Double, or else …" she said.'

'Or else what?' asked Shepherd.

'She said, "I'll start a new company. The two new bands will come to me; in time most of your old bands will come to me too. You're finished, James." That's what she said.' McNab's voice became stronger. 'I started MMI fifteen years ago. I built the company. I couldn't let her end it all. Not someone like her.'

'So you invited her for a walk on the beach,' said Shepherd.

'Yes,' said McNab. 'I told her I was sure we could agree something. I went out through the back door so no-one saw us together. Then I met her outside the front of the hotel.'

He pushed his fingers through his hair and spoke again. 'I told her I wanted to talk about it. I tried one last time. I said I'd give her fifty per cent more money. "Double or nothing," she said. She laughed at me. That made me so angry. She turned her back on me to look out to sea. There was a piece of wood on the beach. I hit her with it. Just once. She fell. It was all over.'

'Then you took her room key, went to her room and took the laptop,' said Shepherd.

'Yes,' said McNab. 'I went in and out through the back door again. I took the laptop out to that old garage behind the hotel. I broke it up into pieces with a large stone and hid it.' His head went down.

'Fox,' said Shepherd. 'Get another officer and take Mr McNab to the police station.' She looked at the other people in the room. 'OK. You all need to put in writing what you've done over the last twenty-four hours. Then you're free to go.'

Fifteen minutes later Shepherd and Webb were sitting in the bar. There was a half-empty glass of red wine in front of Shepherd, and an orange juice in front of Webb. Shepherd's fingers were playing with the memory stick.

'When did I say I wanted someone to look at the back door?' she asked.

'You didn't,' replied Webb.

'Good for you,' said Shepherd. 'I like having a sergeant who uses his brain.'

'Well, I knew the killer didn't have much time to decide how to kill Engel,' said Webb. 'I just thought it would be a good idea to look for fingerprints on the back door. I mean, nobody has gloves with them in September anyway.'

Shepherd smiled.

'It's lucky for us too that Claudia Engel put everything

OCT 1 8 2011

onto the memory stick and left it at reception,' said Webb. 'And that you thought to ask them about it.'

'It's not lucky at all,' said Shepherd.

'What do you mean?' asked Webb.

'It's not her memory stick,' said Shepherd. 'I borrowed it from reception just before I talked to that lot.'

'But the writing on the envelope ...' said Webb.

'Engel wrote her name at reception when she arrived two days ago. I thought I did quite a good job of making it look the same.'

'But ... ' began Webb. 'You mean ...'

'That's right,' she said. 'McNab believed we knew everything, but actually we didn't.'

Shepherd took a drink of her wine.

'So what was on her computer?' asked Webb. 'What was so important?'

'I have no idea,' said Shepherd and laughed. 'If we're lucky, McNab will tell us. But if he doesn't, that's OK too. He's told us that he killed Engel. That's the important thing. And from the look on his face he didn't bring any gloves with him. So we'll probably have his fingerprints too.'

Webb drank some of his orange juice and looked at Shepherd. She really wasn't the usual kind of police inspector.

'We found the murderer ...' Shepherd looked at her watch '... in under twelve hours. I call that a good day's work. Well done us!'

Webb smiled.

'Right,' said Shepherd, standing up and finishing her drink. 'I'm going to give this memory stick back to reception. Mine's another glass of red wine.'

48